How to Write
Powerful Letters
of
Recommendation

Susan Whalley, M.Ed.

Library of Congress Catalog Card No. 00-106545

ISBN 1-930572-05-0

Printing (Last Digit)

    10   9   8   7   6   5

Published and Distributed by—
Marco Products, Inc./Educational Media Corporation®
1443 Old York Road
Warminster, PA 18974
1-800-448-2197

www.marcoproducts.com

Production Editor—
Don. L. Sorenson

Graphic Design—
Earl Sorenson

Table of Contents

Acknowledgments

My deepest appreciation goes to the students I have been privileged to care for over the last twenty years. There is no greater mystery to me than the development of the human being over time, and no greater enjoyment than being a witness to this mystery. I have loved knowing them all.

I also want to express my deepest gratitude to the Billerica Public Schools, Shawsheen Valley Regional School District, Swampscott Public Schools, and Lunenburg Public Schools for employing me during this lifetime and enabling me to fulfill my mission to encourage and guide youth.

This guide could not have been produced without the help of admissions officers I have come to know over the years. I have also learned many things from conversations and interviews with representatives from The College Board, Brown University, Boston College, Boston University, Harvard College, and The George Washington University.

About the Author

Susan Whalley, a native New Yorker, has been a guidance counselor in the Greater Boston area for over twenty years. She lives in the woods of Carlisle, Massachusetts with her husband David, their children, and Chocolate Labrador Retriever, Mugsy.

When not writing letters on behalf of her students, she devotes herself to their well-being in many other ways. She is also a member of SGI-USA, a Buddhist organization devoted to world peace.

Susan loves taking care of her family, her wonderful friends, and gardening. When not doing these things, she's "on the road" seeing the world.

Thoughts on Letter Writing

How can an educator write a powerful letter of recommendation for all students whose post-secondary plans require one? Our days are filled with many duties; therefore, much of this work needs to be done after-hours.

Many of my colleagues labor over this kind of letter writing because when they do have time to write the letter, they are tired from a day's work, so they cannot give the letter the zest and attention they would like.

Writing a letter of recommendation requires vitality, concentration, and knowledge of the student. Educators have all three, or they could not work in the profession. The task is to put all three together at one time to produce a letter.

Some schools give their faculty members a professional day off-site if they are called upon to write many letters each year. This does not need to go to contract negotiations. If your school places a value on putting together the best admissions package for students, an informal arrangement between the faculty member and administrator could be arranged.

Some schools have each senior delineate in the fall which teacher they will be asking to write a letter for him or her. This prevents a student from having four or five letters written by staff when one would suffice. On the rare occasion that two teacher letters plus the counselor letter are required, the rules can be bent. This same system can also work if a student needs a reference from a science teacher for one school and an English teacher for another school.

Some high schools create a team of teachers to brainstorm together about a student they have had in common who is applying to an extremely competitive school. The information from the session is then condensed into a letter signed by a member of the team.

Recommendation letters can be positive, or they can be glowing and electric. Which type of letter will help your students gain acceptance to their desired program? *The one that helps them to stand out from the others!* We all rose to the positions of responsibility we enjoy because, somewhere along the line, people wrote letters of recommendation for us. Now it's our turn to return the favor.

How can you muster the required enthusiasm? This book is meant to help you to jump-start your own thinking process. To make the reading of the letter samples more fun, I have changed the names of the students to protect their privacy. Instead of generic names, enjoy trying to figure out the mystery guest. While creating the pseudonyms, I realized the new name puzzles have a deeper purpose. The purpose is to remind us that the young women and men about whom we write will someday be strong, influential adults in their own arenas of life.

To Begin

- Just start. Do not put it off. Every day is as strenuous as every other day. Many feel "Tomorrow I'll have the time and energy." This is a comforting thought, but it can add to a buildup of anxiety as the deadline for the finished letter nears.

- Get the power. From where? Power comes from the sincerity and vision of the writer. By allowing yourself to embrace the task before you, not rush it or begrudge it, you can really enjoy your process and your product. The moments of your life that you devote to this (or anything) are yours. The project itself is a private pact between you and the admissions officer you may never know. For this reason, approach the task as a creative journey to enjoy and the letter will take on a heart and a tone that is rich and powerful.

- Close the door, refuse phone calls (except emergencies of course), and eliminate possible distractions. Sometimes we can sabotage our letter writing as we unconsciously welcome a distraction. Then we are back to step number one.

- Sit quietly at the table, desk, or computer and look at the blank page facing you. Visualize a full page of text you are proud of having written.

- Picture the student in your mind. Focus on the image of this person. Try to penetrate the core of this person's character or essence. What did this student look like at birth? Age two? Four? Six? Sitting in the grade four classroom? Grade six? The first day of high school? Try to see the person as the bundle of promise that the parent sees. Unfortunately, maybe not all parents feel this way about their children, but, as a trusted caretaker, can you?

- Once you have this deep feeling/insight into the student, imagine that person five years from now, then ten, then thirty. The person is a capable, confident adult. Picture the person in the adult work environment, the home environment.

- Brainstorm adjectives about the student (see the *List of Descriptive Words and Phrases* at the end of this book for help). Write the adjectives down, then brainstorm anecdotes that you could include. Then, brainstorm attributes about the student. This will give you a great foundation to begin.

Now you are ready to write.

You may simply begin with the *Letter of Recommendation for: Albert Jacobs,* which is crisper than: To whom it may concern.

Begin your letter by describing in what capacity you know the student and how long you have been acquainted. I like to use the student's full formal name in the first paragraph, and often wrap up the last paragraph using the full, formal name. From the samples in this book, you will notice I often use the student's nickname so the writing will flow more naturally and the reader can get a truer sense of the student's personality.

Describe the person's essential character based on the deep thought you have given at the start. Let the words flow, don't edit the letter as you write it.

Include specific anecdotes about the student in a clear, concise, yet comfortable fashion. This will help to keep the reader's attention and make your student's application stand out from those of others. What makes this student special?

Teachers can describe *in detail* a challenging project or unit that the student participated in and the outcome. This is a great way to beef-up a letter that might seem too slim. This is also a good technique if you have not come to know the student too well.

Make every attempt to state facts:

No: "James performed well in my psychology course and was one of the best students in the class. He will likely be a good teacher."

Yes: "In a research project (describe the project) based on these observations, I predict that he will be an outstanding high school teacher."

Comment on how the above information relates to the student's choice of college program or job opening.

Stress the potential of the individual and why that person is qualified for the job or admission to the college.

Write about how you feel about the student and what was contributed to your classroom, your experience, *your* life.

If it will help the student, it is fine to share with the reader how students, staff, and administration feel about this student. This person will probably earn the same kind of respect in the college environment.

The reader will want to know how the applicant will add to the life and the culture of the college. What sets this student apart from others?

If you have visited the campus (or if you went to school there), it is a great idea to mention that you feel this person would be a good match for the school and list some reasons why. Will the student add to participation in the classroom? Be a good role model? Lead others in activities?

Include any irregularities that may have negatively influenced this person's life and caused his or her record to suffer (death in the family, other tragedy, new family responsibilities).

Does the student have a true love of learning? Does he or she take challenging courses? Did the student take advantage of any programs that demonstrate a desire for more opportunity than just taking classes at your school? Did the student take advantage of classes at a local college, summer internships, or adventures that enabled growth in new directions? Is there continuity in the interest area of the student over time? Does he or she do extra projects or just required work? Is he or she excited by the work or just diligent and dutiful?

After your letter is written, proofread and edit until it is a letter you feel represents the student and will be captivating to the reader.

How long should it be?

Letters are generally one typed page.

If you think it is warranted, you may provide a different letter for each school the student is applying to, or a generic letter. For the most selective schools, it is better to provide a letter designed exclusively for that school. Then, remove the particular school's name from the letter and create a more generic one for the student's file. This letter can be used again and again by the student, as it will remain in the file at your school.

Things to consider:

When the student requests a letter of recommendation from you...

Do you have to write one?

If you are overextended, you can tell that to the student. Teachers can post a notice in the classroom indicating a deadline by which all requests for letters will be taken. Also handy is a notice indicating how much time the student needs to give you to write the letter before it will need to be mailed.

Ask yourself if you know the student well enough to write a helpful recommendation. What are your impressions of that student? Can you be honest in writing this letter? If you have reservations, let the student know. If you fear your credibility will suffer if you write a positive letter and don't include weaknesses you feel the reader should know about, you can include those weaknesses and still write a positive recommendation.

If a student has been difficult to get to know, and I haven't yet found the key, I often write about how this person will grow in maturity in the future, has yet to blossom, or how the student has high hopes for a fresh, new start. I let the admissions officer take it from there, from between the lines.

It is a good idea to keep a copy of the letter for your files. Employers may call to clarify information, the same student may come back to ask for another letter, or it may help you get started when you have to do one for somebody else. Also ask the student to let you know how he or she did. Writing letters of recommendation can be time consuming, but with practice, you will soon develop your own style and system.

Ask for an informal resume of interests and activities.

Students may think that their teachers and counselors are all-seeing and all-knowing. Therefore, some are surprised to learn we might write a better letter for them if we had a (typed) list of their interests and activities for reference.

Set up an appointment to meet with the student. Ask the student to bring the list to the meeting. This will provide you with information about the student's background, in addition to an awareness of other areas of his or her life.

Use the meeting to ask the student about his or her specific purpose, (e.g., "Why are you going on to college?" Is there one area of interest that you have had throughout your life?).

The student should give you the name and complete address of the person you'll be writing to, along with the date by which the letter is needed.

You may want to invite parents to contribute their written thoughts to you when you send out the school newsletter in the fall. This is great for enhancing the relationship between the school and the home. Teachers can access this information through the guidance department if that is a likely site.

How much notice?

I tell students they can expect the letter to be completed within ten working days.

Two weeks from the date they requested a letter, they can check to see if the letter has been deposited in the file, or if they need to expedite it.

To waive or not to waive?

Most colleges include a space for the student to declare if she or he chooses to waive rights to review the supporting documents (checklists and letters) sent with the application. The student's choice to waive these rights, therefore, should be apparent to you on the form the student provides to you.

I let students know that the admissions officers reading their applications will see them differently if they are sure the letters of recommendation were written in a totally candid manner. I *advise* them to waive their rights, but I also tell them they can do as they wish. I let them know that the reader may have, in the back of his or her mind, the thought that the writer may have been less than candid because it was felt that the letter would be scrutinized (criticized) by "interested parties."

Your reputation on the line.

College admissions officers become familiar with the schools in their territory. I am concerned with my credibility over time. If I write letters that overinflate the attributes of the student, in a few years, who will believe me?

It is always possible to bring out students' character strengths and humanity, even if their scholarly performance is weak. This is why some quiet moments meditating on the inner essence of each student is important. Then, you need a good supply of adjectives to splash around. (See the list of *Descriptive Words and Phrases* at the end of the book).

In the section entitled *The Hardest Ones to Write,* I have included examples. Not all students let themselves be known to the adults at school. If I cannot think of what to write, I will talk to a few of the student's teachers, increase my font a notch, and stick with characteristics of the student's personality.

Wrapping it up.

You can:

- Recommend with enthusiasm
- Wholeheartedly recommend
- Recommend without reservation
- Recommend
- Let the admissions officers know that you welcome their call if they have follow-up questions about a student.

It is extremely rare for an admissions officer to receive a letter that is not positive. Don't worry about seeming too positive—that's why the student asked you in the first place. You may, however, need to adjust what qualities you are being positive about.

My goal is to offer a positive letter. If I feel that the student will be a background player at college, that's fine. The world would be unlivable if everyone was a "star."

If not on your letterhead, include your title and telephone number or address where you can be reached.

Things to keep in mind:

Organize the information
- Performance in class
- Specific examples of work
- Evidence of study habits
- Behavior outside of class
- Anecdotal information

What to Include:
- Ability to communicate
- Intelligence
- Competitiveness
- Self-confidence
- Willingness to accept responsibility
- Direction
- Initiative
- Ability to handle conflict
- Leadership
- Self-knowledge
- Energy level
- Appropriate vocational skills
- Imagination
- Goal achievement
- Flexibility
- Interpersonal skills

Avoid bland words
- Nice
- Reasonable
- Good
- Decent
- Fairly
- Satisfactory

Use powerful words
- Articulate
- Intelligent
- Expressive
- Cooperative
- Dependable
- Effective
- Observant
- Creative
- Imaginative
- Mature
- Sophisticated
- Significant
- Efficient
- Assertive
- Innovative

Do's and Don'ts
- All letters should be typed and proofread.
- Admissions officers report receiving identical letters from a counselor who merely changed the name of the student.
- Keep a copy.
- Have fun and write great letters!

They Take the Lead

Recommendation for Jonathan Crandee

As his track coach, I have known Jonathan Crandee for three years. He is extremely well liked at school and in the community. Jon is a wholesome, well-rounded young man who has outstanding abilities in both the math and verbal areas. He also has exerted himself in athletics.

Jon has taken a leadership role as captain of the track teams at our school over the years. From this experience, he gained valuable skills. He not only encouraged and inspired others, but he created working teams. This, I feel, is a crucial aspect for success in the coming century. His involvement in track teams, the math team and the electronics club have been diverse experiences, ones where Jon has made great contributions while representing our school.

Jon's family is extremely supportive and loving. He has been raised to be a wonderful human being. What strikes me most about Jon is his sincerity. He is humble, considerate and mature. He is easy to talk with, unaffected by his own gifts—one of the best individuals this graduating class has to offer.

I enthusiastically recommend Jon for any program he aspires to explore. His innate abilities, as well as his solid, honest, trustworthy character, indicates that he will excel and make a rich contribution in his own right to your class of 20XX.

Sincerely,

"Jon has taken a leadership role as captain of the track teams at our school over the years. From this experience, he gained valuable skills. He not only encouraged and inspired others, but he created working teams."

Recommendation for Charles Berrie

I am pleased to offer this letter of recommendation on behalf of Charles Berrie. I have known Charlie for three years in my role as the advisor to peer mediators. He is a wonderful person, a delight to know, with an ebullient spirit and a deep humanity.

You can tell by looking at Charlie's transcript that he has undisputed academic talents. He also is an able musician, and he has devoted himself to the school band and the jazz band all four years here. He also is a volunteer peer mediator and peer counselor, a responsibility which has called him to undergo training over the years, and to provide assistance to fellow students who might have a need to talk things over with a peer, or to receive academic help. In this capacity, Charlie also has worked with students in the primary grades, providing classroom sessions on drug abuse and other social issues.

"....he has undisputed academic talents. He also is an able musician, and he has devoted himself to the school band... enables all those with whom he comes in contact to feel at ease."

Charlie has a quiet confidence, and he enables all those with whom he comes in contact to feel at ease. He has a great sense of humor and is mature and compassionate. He comes from a close family that always has taken a strong interest in his development as a well-rounded person. His family upbringing is a major reason why he is the excellent individual that I have had the pleasure to know.

I have absolute confidence that Charlie will excel in college and that he will make a great contribution to your incoming class. Please feel free to call me with any questions you may have.

Sincerely,

Recommendation for Richard Curtain

I am delighted to write this letter of recommendation on behalf of Richard Curtain. Richard is a serious student who cares deeply about the world around him. He has extended himself into his school and the larger community more than any other student with whom I have worked during my career. He is modest, self-effacing, sensitive, yet strong and has a deep sense of dedication. The enclosed credentials support my statement.

Richard's father suffered from kidney disease, lingered painfully and died last year. Richard moved through this loss and the ensuing grief and adjustments with grace. He took the lead as the "man" of the house, caring for his mother and younger sister. He held down the fort each evening as his mother worked the late shift to support her family. Richard never wanted to use this loss as an excuse for problems concentrating in his classes, and he pulled out of his junior year with a good academic performance.

Richard is a very positive role model for others. He has worked seriously in our theater groups. He was consistently elected by his peers to represent them in a variety of capacities. The faculty of our school has the highest regard for Richard. They selected him to represent us at a regional student council conference.

Richard's full potential has yet to be realized. He tackled his entire high school career while his father was in and out of the hospital. He endured stress and grief in his family and lived with his own pain. I believe his academic grades, overall, have been "depressed" because of this constant strain. His SAT scores promise that the best is yet to come. I recommend Richard Curtain with enthusiasm. He will make tremendous contributions to your campus environment.

Sincerely,

"Richard is a serious student who cares deeply about the world around him. He has extended himself into his school and the larger community more than any other student with whom I have worked during my career. He is modest, self-effacing, sensitive, yet strong and has a deep sense of dedication."

Recommendation for Katherine Tourick

Katherine Tourick is always on the move. She is a high-energy person with great enthusiasm and a strong, uplifting personality. She is sensitive, a young woman of humor and responsiveness. Katie keeps her eye on her goals, is a positive influence on those around her and is, at the same time, calm and confident.

Katie has terrific interpersonal skills. I have watched these blossom steadily over the years. This young woman, as a student council representative, its vice-president and this year its president, is an effective lobbyist between our administration and the student body. She has served both extremely well. Her positive outlook and unflagging tact have enabled her to walk this thin diplomatic line with grace. She also was an effective and valued negotiator on issues important to our students.

> *"Katie... is an effective lobbyist between our administration and the student body. She has served both extremely well. Her positive outlook and unflagging tact have enabled her to walk this thin diplomatic line with grace."*

The leadership skills Katie exhibits have developed as a result of the efforts she has made. She is vice president of her class, captain of many of our teams and she has had numerous leadership-camp training experiences. She also has worked as a leadership trainer and has earned the trust of her peers, being elected to positions on and off the field.

Extra-curricular and co-curricular activities aside, Katie also has established an extremely strong academic record, excelling in our most rigorous courses. She is equally talented in the math/science and verbal/social science areas. Abilities like hers are rare.

I wholeheartedly recommend Katie Tourick for admission to your school. She will contribute tremendously to the academic excellence of the classes she chooses, as well as the activities that create a meaningful student culture on campus. As a graduate of your school, I see her as the quintessential student, advancing toward the next millennium with gifts that will be enhanced even more by the opportunities that lie ahead.

Sincerely,

Recommendation for Jane Truedahl

I am writing on behalf of Jane Truedahl as the advisor to our school literary magazine. Last year Jane was the assistant editor, and this year she has taken on the responsibility of editor.

Working with Jane and knowing Jane have been one of the greatest pleasures of my career. This girl radiates enthusiasm and life. She is fun, conscientious, bright, capable, a great friend to her peers and an organized student. She is mature and involved. Jane also is aware of social issues in the world around her. She sees how these affect her daily life and works at creating change in her environment.

Whether through her role as a peer counselor at school, a National Honor Society peer tutor, a member of SADD, a lifeguard during the summers or editor of the school magazine, Jane instinctively knows how to engage those around her. She is genuine, optimistic, kind and has enormous energy. She is also embracing. Even when agonizing over deadlines, Jane keeps her cool and her sense of humor. She is able to get her message across, and is always strict with herself.

> *"Jane... is genuine, optimistic, kind, and has enormous energy. She is also embracing. Even when agonizing over deadlines, Jane keeps her cool and her sense of humor. She is able to get her message across, and is always strict with herself."*

Jane is concerned with others' welfare: How will they get home from afternoon meetings? Are they overworked? How do we train the next editor? How can I best utilize the talent we have and bring in others? She is connected to all different types of people, different age groups, with different interests. She manages this through her powerful and endearing life force.

Everyone likes this girl! She is a natural leader, the best her generation has to offer. Jane is the kind of student you never want to see graduate, because her life adds so much to the school in so many ways.

Jane is dedicated. She is sincere. Whatever she sets out to do, she accomplishes. She has always opted for the hardest classes offered, even though she anticipated a rough road. For example, Jane was one of the only girls in Physics last year and in Calculus this year. She is willing to take risks and works hard to do her best. Jane is also taking a psychology class at our local state college.

Jane will excel at any program of studies she chooses and add energy and power to your student body. I recommend her enthusiastically.

Sincerely,

Recommendation for Jane Paddems

I am happy to offer this letter of recommendation on behalf of Jane Paddems. I have known Jane for three years as her guidance counselor.

Jane is a wholesome, bright, energetic young woman. She also is confident, respectful, and thoughtful. A terrific optimist, Jane has had to deal with the chronic poor health of both of hers parents for years, with their recurrent hospitalizations and outpatient treatment. Jane has risen to each occasion as a stable force in her family, looking after her younger brother and not caving in to despair. The stresses she has faced are more than most high school students must face—the issues of life and death.

Jane always has selected a challenging set of courses. Sticking with the hard sciences and continuing in math, Jane would rather work to do her best in challenging classes than take the easy route. This deserves recognition. Jane is a fighter.

> *"... Jane has had to deal with the chronic poor health of both of hers parents for years, with their recurrent hospitalizations and outpatient treatment. Jane has risen to each occasion as a stable force in her family, looking after her younger brother and not caving in to despair. The stresses she has faced are more than most high school students must face, the issues of life and death."*

The clubs and sports in which Jane has participated have benefited from her participation. She is the epitome of a team player and is well liked by students and staff. Jane has committed herself to activities as a peer counselor, and is the president of the largest high school chapter of Future Business Leaders of America in the region.

Jane has shown strong leadership ability in many different arenas: at home, in clubs and in sports. I believe in Jane and know she will be successful at college and will add tremendously to a student life on campus.

Sincerely,

Pluggers

They Tried Harder

Recommendation for Sarah Pride

I am happy to offer this letter of recommendation on behalf of Sarah Pride. I have known Sarah for three years in my role as the advisor to peer educators.

Sarah is one of the most compassionate and mature students we have. She is serious, conscientious and kind. I admire Sarah for carefully selecting courses in which she is genuinely interested. Though she might not be naturally talented in the areas of math and science, she undertook the challenge of these courses in her junior year. This year, taking courses to help prepare her for a future in elementary education, she also chose to continue with Latin up to Level IV.

Sarah has devoted herself as a peer educator to receive training in working with elementary school students. Her dream is to work with children as a classroom teacher. She has an ability to establish incredible connections with kids. She also has devoted many weeks to training as a peer counselor for the high school to help students who are under stress. She really gives of herself.

Sarah is extremely well liked and maintains her own sense of self, not swayed by others. She also is a sincere and loyal friend.

I recommend Sarah for the Future Teachers of America scholarship with enthusiasm.

Sincerely,

"Sarah has devoted herself as a peer educator to receive training in working with elementary school students. Her dream is to work with children as a classroom teacher. She has an ability to establish incredible connections with kids.... She really gives of herself."

Recommendation for James Barter

It is a pleasure to offer this letter of recommendation for James Barter.

I have known Jim for three years as his guidance counselor.

Jim is a steady and mature young man. He has a strong and deep character, a selfless devotion to others and maturity beyond his years. Academically, he has challenged himself in his selection of courses, taking hard science and mathematics throughout his four years and continuing in Spanish up to Level V.

Although Jim has performed very well here at school, I must mention his work with Habitat for Humanity in Georgia. Through tremendous dedication, teamwork and effort, Jim and his friends raised money to go to a poverty-stricken area of Georgia. There he lived with the poorest of families, fixing roofs, building steps—whatever was needed. This experience has marked a turning point for Jim. His service to others has become a guide for the planning of his future. I admire him very much for this.

Jim is a kind, modest, thoughtful and self-disciplined young man. I have great confidence in him and know that he will excel in his chosen field of study. I recommend him to the Americorps Program without reservation.

Sincerely,

"Through tremendous dedication, teamwork and effort, Jim and his friends raised money to go to a poverty-stricken area of Georgia. There he lived with the poorest of families, fixing roofs, building steps—whatever was needed.... His service to others has become a guide for the planning of his future."

Recommendation for Amelia Soarcart

Amelia Soarcart is a terrific person, a great student, a sincere friend and a vibrant spirit. I have known Amelia as her guidance counselor for three years. I have been impressed with the strength of her character, the drive and motivation that she uses to fuel her pursuits and the passion she has to do well.

Although she is the only child of divorced parents, she remains unspoiled and connected to both parents in a very positive way. The direction they have given her over the years has been firm and consistent. I believe Amelia has a great sense of confidence because of the evenhanded and loving way she has been raised.

Amelia is very hard-working, focused and interested in everything she undertakes. She is thorough, takes time after school or during lunch to work at her studies and has a deep sense of commitment. What impresses me so much is her pursuit of the hard sciences and math. She has taken every science course our school offers. In math last year she finished with a course in Analysis. She is equally talented in the verbal areas. This spring she will be taking extra courses at our local state college in creative writing.

Amelia is extremely likable, connected to others and mature. I know she will excel at college and will be a leader for other young women and men in whatever activity or program she undertakes.

Sincerely,

"Although she is the only child of divorced parents, she remains unspoiled and connected to both parents in a very positive way. The direction they have given her over the years has been firm and consistent. I believe that Amelia has a great sense of confidence because of the evenhanded and loving way she has been raised."

Recommendation for Bonnie Tate

I am happy to offer this letter of recommendation on behalf of Bonnie Tate. As her coach, I have known Bonnie for three years.

Bonnie always has challenged herself in some of the most difficult courses our school offers. As you can see from her transcript, she has continued to work hard and improve over the years. She is highly motivated and enthusiastic. Her teachers find her a terrific asset in the classroom. I asked Bonnie why she wanted to go on to advanced biology and calculus in her senior year, even though she would not need those courses to be an elementary school teacher. She said she believed it was important for her to keep expanding her base of knowledge. I admire her for that.

Bonnie is extremely well liked and maintains her own sense of self. Others do not sway her. She also is a sincere and loyal friend. She participates in many activities and clubs at school.

"Bonnie is extremely well liked and maintains her own sense of self. Others do not sway her. She is also a sincere and loyal friend. She participates in many activities and clubs at school."

Bonnie's dream is to work with children as a classroom teacher. She is able to establish trusting relationships with the children with whom she has worked. She volunteers as a referee for a second and third grade softball team and fourth and fifth grade soccer team each weekend. An active person, Bonnie devotes herself to skateboarding and tennis. She is the star of our high school's field hockey team.

I recommend Bonnie to your program without reservation. I had a chance to visit your school last fall. I met with students and faculty during the counselor tour and dinner. I can easily envision Bonnie blossoming in your warm campus atmosphere, and know that she would make a great contribution to your school's student life, as well.

Sincerely,

Recommendation for Thomas Redison

I am very happy to be able to write this letter of recommendation on behalf of Thomas Redison. Tom and I have known each other for three years; I am his guidance counselor.

Tom is a success story. This young man is one of the finest we will ever graduate from this high school. He wins the prize for hard work and diligence and for facing his obstacles squarely and overcoming them. Yes, he has struggled with language-based learning disabilities. To see his selection of courses for his senior year and his progress to date, one would never guess at the climb he has made to overcome any weakness in his learning style.

His love of biology and his goals for the future have enabled him to do well in Advanced Biology. Similarly, he holds his own in Trig/Algebra III and is taking a very demanding social science course—Behavioral Science—and is doing well. Add to this English and various electives, and note that Tom is earning better grades now than ever before with no support from our special services staff.

"Tom is a success story. This young man is one of the finest we will ever graduate from this high school. He wins the prize for hard work and diligence and for facing his obstacles squarely and overcoming them. Yes, he has struggled with language-based learning disabilities."

Tom is also a sensitive, kind, human being. He has great humility and, at the same time, deep confidence in himself. I know with certainty that Tom will succeed in his goal to serve others in the realm of sports psychology. He will also be a solid, mature student who will be a great example to others. I recommend him to your technical college without reservation.

Sincerely,

Recommendation for Judith Farland

I am happy to offer this letter of recommendation on behalf of Judith Farland. Judy has been a student of mine for three years; I am her guidance counselor.

Judy has had a bumpy road throughout high school. She has met each of her challenges beautifully. I met her during a time of trouble that you will read about in her essay. Frightened and feeling alone with many big decisions to make, Judy grew up quickly in a very short period of time. She took a couple of months off from school. Work was sent home from her teachers for her to complete. I was the liaison for this process. First of all, without exception, Judy's teachers rallied around her to support her and encourage her. Judy turned in all of her work and kept pace with her classes from afar. Reading over the assignments before I handed them in for her, I was always struck by her thoroughness, sense of self-respect and the depth with which she completed her projects and homework.

"Judy has had a bumpy road through high school. She has met each of her challenges beautifully. I met her during a time of trouble that you will read about in her essay. Frightened and feeling alone with many big decisions to make, Judy grew up quickly in a very short period of time."

After most of the personal issues in Judy's life had passed, the dust settled and I have gotten to know a person of depth and who has become quite mature for her age. Judy has tremendous potential. Her academic profile shows a difficult time in math, and she was seen by the special education teachers in middle school. Independent of an educational plan in high school, she maintained her efforts.

I have full confidence that Judy will do well at college, and that the best is yet to come as she fine-tunes her area of interest and takes related course work. Please feel free to call on me if there is any further information I can supply.

Sincerely,

Recommendation for Rachel Karlson

Rachel Karlson is a self-sufficient young woman. Her quiet disposition belies a deep enthusiasm for the many endeavors of her daily life.

Rachel is a skilled artist, a team player on and off the field, and a loyal friend to her classmates. Without pretense, this student works steadily at all her subjects, involves herself in extracurricular activities and maintains a good-humored approach to life.

Last year Rachel's father died after a long illness. Although she has dealt with her grief in a private way, I was surprised to see her never use this great loss as an excuse to fall in her studies. This takes an inner resolve that is difficult to fathom. Rachel not only kept up her excellent academic performance, but also continued to represent our school in cross-country track, field hockey and a variety of other clubs and activities.

> *"...a young woman with talent, strength, positive outlook and compassion. She has tremendous gifts to offer others and will "light-up," in her own quiet way, the students and staff around her. She is confident, caring and forward looking."*

I see Rachel as a young woman with talent, strength, positive outlook and compassion. She has tremendous gifts to offer others and will "light-up," in her own quiet way, the students and staff around her. She is confident, caring and forward looking. As a graduate of Bilner College, I recommend her without reservation, knowing her inner qualities and depth will enhance the already wonderful student culture at Bilner.

Sincerely,

Recommendation for Lauren LaCall

I am happy to offer this letter of recommendation for Lauren LaCall. I have known her for three years as her art teacher.

Lauren has kept up a steady, strong effort in all her studies and hobbies over the years. She is a plugger.

Lauren: mature, quiet, serious, a good head on her shoulders. Her interest in animals has led her to volunteer at a local animal shelter for the past four years. Her goal to go on in veterinary studies has been paramount in her mind (and heart) since I've known her. Equally durable is the strength of character she has achieved as a result of her effort in acting. Her summers have been spent exploring this talent and performing at community theaters. Lauren is also a capable student of art and a member of the National Art Honor Society.

Peers and teachers respect Lauren. She is strong in so many areas. She is so sincere in the projects that she undertakes that I am confident that she will do well in any program of studies she chooses.

Sincerely,

"Her goal to go on in veterinary studies has been paramount in her mind (and heart) since I've known her. Equally durable is the strength of character she has achieved as a result of her effort in acting."

Recommendation for Lucille Brawl

I am delighted to write on behalf of Lucille Brawl. Lucille is a serious and independent student. She lives from the depths of her life, and is not concerned with superficial matters. She is also very likable and sincere. A good friend to others, Lucille works well with many different types of people, is kind and broad-minded.

Teachers have loved having Lucille in their classes, primarily because of the insights she shares based on her depth and seriousness and her ability to sustain focus during class lessons. She sets the tone for class discussions because of this. She is an extremely hard worker and is very bright. Lucille is committed to developing herself toward the future.

"Teachers have loved having Lucille in their classes, primarily because of the insights she shares based on her depth and seriousness and her ability to sustain focus during class lessons. She sets the tone for class discussions because of this."

Each year since eighth grade, Lucille has continued with French and has taken the advanced science for her grade level, culminating with Advanced Biology. Because our only other offering is Physics, Lucille's way of continuing in science was to take on Environmental Studies, in which she is excelling.

I heartily recommend Lucille for the Student Achievement Award Scholarship because she has what it takes to be totally successful— intelligence, perseverance, focus and great character.

Sincerely,

Recommendation for Benjamin Conklin

I am pleased to offer this letter of recommendation on behalf of Benjamin Conklin. As his dramatics teacher, I have known Ben for three years.

Ben is a very likable young man, mature and polite. I also find him to be an extremely hard worker. He has been an asset in the classroom, participating in discussions with enthusiasm and asking pertinent questions. He is conscientious in his studies. Teachers really enjoy having Ben in their classes.

I have watched Ben develop a greater sense of confidence over the years. He has worked hard to compensate for some attention deficit and possible mild dyslexia. As a junior, Ben won the underclassmen's award for perseverance in Spanish.

"...an extremely hard worker. He has been an asset in the classroom, participating in discussions with enthusiasm and asking pertinent questions. He is conscientious in his studies. Teachers really enjoy having Ben in their classes."

I admire Ben for the devoted activity he has provided his class over the years. His talents and interests range from acting in class plays, serving on the varsity basketball team, membership in the Art Club, creating a class video scrapbook and designing the class logo. Ben also has taken martial arts classes for years and has earned advanced standing.

I find Ben to be a one-of-a-kind person. Because he has had to work harder than others to get his grades, he has learned tenacity and humility. At the same time he is to be admired for the inner reserve he has developed in order to be successful. These qualities enable me to believe that Ben will be successful at anything he undertakes. I recommend him without reservation.

Sincerely,

Letter of Recommendation for Alvin Doar

I am happy to write this letter of recommendation on behalf of Alvin Doar. Al is a serious student who cares deeply about the world around him. His real passion, besides basketball, is social science. I have seen him in debate, helped him to shape his academic program each year and worked through some difficult times with this young man.

Al's mother suffered from cancer, lingered painfully, and died last year in May. Al moved through this loss and the ensuing grief and adjustments with grace. He helped to care for his younger brother. He never wanted to use this loss as an excuse for problems concentrating in classes, and pulled out of his junior year with a strong academic performance.

Al's full potential is yet to be realized. His entire high school career was endured with the tragedy I described, with stress and grief in his family and with his own pain. I feel his academic grades, overall, have been "depressed" because of this constant strain. His SAT scores promise that the best is yet to come. I recommend Alvin without reservation.

Sincerely,

> *"Al's full potential is yet to be realized. His entire high school career was endured with the tragedy I described, with stress and grief in his family and with his own pain. I feel his academic grades, overall, have been "depressed" because of this constant strain."*

Recommendation for Diana Cross

Diana Cross is an excellent student. She has undertaken a demanding selection of courses each year and made an impact in each class through enthusiastic participation and natural curiosity. She is trustworthy, caring and sensitive and has the highest ethical standards.

A go-getter, Diana is fun, creative and also serious. Her record indicates a broad range of activities and interests in high school. She has devoted herself to each challenge and kept her numerous and varied commitments. She also broke our school record for push-ups—65 in a minute! That is Diana—a winner.

I recommend Diana Cross for this scholarship with enthusiasm. She will contribute much as a young woman who has a good head on her shoulders and a focused, purposeful attitude.

Sincerely,

"A go-getter, Diana is fun, creative and also serious. Her record indicates a broad range of activities and interests in high school. She has devoted herself to each challenge and kept her numerous and varied commitments."

They March to a Different Drummer

Recommendation for John Brennan

I have known John Brennan for almost three years. He is a tremendous spirit, a great intellect and an original thinker. When I see John I am filled with delight, for I know whatever the content of our encounter, I will be enlivened and enriched because of it. He sparkles, is full of surprises and is open and free inside. He is unjaded and without pretense.

John enjoys and solicits intellectual connection. He was once in a dispute with a close friend about the inner workings of one of the characters in Arthur Miller's *The Crucible.* He loves learning, reading and simply being. John seems completely comfortable with himself and has a terrific ability to laugh at himself, yet he also takes issues very seriously. John worked with our staff last year to create a successful workshop to recognize and celebrate diversity. He responds with action when he reads articles in newspapers and magazines about worthy causes. He strongly follows his inner voice with courage.

"…. a tremendous intellect and an original thinker. When I see John I am filled with delight, for I know whatever the content of our encounter, I will be enlivened and enriched because of it. He sparkles, is full of surprises and is open and free inside. He is unjaded and without pretense."

His desire to branch out past the confines of our course offerings, caused him to lead the effort to enable all students to be able to take college courses, get credit and adjust high school course requirements according to the out-of-school course load. Although he was told of our school policy, he felt it would be a hardship for students to take a full course load and additional courses at a nearby state college. John challenged the policy with our principal, superintendent and school committee. In the end, the policy was changed to accommodate an adjusted course load.

Each year I have worked with John to create his schedule. He, more than any other student, has been adamant about taking the most challenging courses possible. Although mathematics was not his strongest area, John insisted on taking Analysis as a junior because he wanted the challenge. He has always chosen the most challenging courses we have to offer and has taken our most accelerated program.

John also gives generously of his time and talents. He volunteers at our local library regularly to tell stories to younger children. He also volunteers at our local hospital and donates his time at our local senior center giving piano recitals.

I am confident that he will excel in your highly competitive academic environment. I know he will bring tremendous life and spirit to the class of 20XX. Please let me know if I can provide more information to support his candidacy for admission.

Sincerely,

They March to a Different Drummer

Recommendation for Veronica Blake

I have known Veronica Blake for one and a half years as her guidance counselor. I find her to be a serious student with a unique world view. Veronica exudes confidence and has outstanding verbal skills. She is quite an individual and has always demanded the most from the time she has invested in her education. When she left our high school at the end of her sophomore year, Veronica found the educational offerings at her new high school not up to her rigorous standards and opted to be "home schooled" instead.

Upon her return to school this month, Veronica arranged a most challenging course selection, but we were unable to accommodate her in AP English, so she remained in a standard college program. Veronica is determined to prepare for and to take the AP test in the spring, however. When this girl is determined, nothing stops her!

Veronica has exerted herself over the years in band and chorus, and was the lone female in wood shop as a sophomore. Veronica is a courageous person. She has tremendous drive and a strong inner voice. I know she will do well at college. She will grow enormously from the experience of schooling in your excellent academic environment.

Sincerely,

> *"....a serious student with a unique world view. Veronica exudes confidence and has outstanding verbal skills. She is quite an individual and has always demanded the most from the time she has invested in her education."*

Mature Beyond Their Years

Mature Beyond Their Years

Recommendation for Paul Crewman

Paul Crewman is an incredible human being. You will see from his transcript that he is talented academically. From his resume you will note that he is well rounded, a leader and generous with his time.

Here is a young man who is a capable team player in the sports arena and has taken leadership as co-captain on the soccer team. He has consistently shown an interest in developing his leadership skills still further by attending many conferences and workshops over the years.

Something that is not readily apparent from the information he provided with his application is the depth of his expertise in the area of art appreciation. He and his father have been working together for about ten years and Paul has become an astute businessman in the arts. His interest in this area has brought him in contact with adults and has enabled him to travel extensively on the East Coast.

Paul is very mature for his age. He is intelligent and a hard worker.

He is extremely likable and sincere. Paul exudes humility. This enables others to be comfortable with him. I have enjoyed knowing Paul these past three years and recommend him enthusiastically for your program.

Sincerely,

"...depth of... expertise in the area of art appreciation. He and his father have been working together for about ten years and Paul has become an astute businessman in the arts. His interest in this area has brought him in contact with adults and has enabled him to travel extensively on the East Coast."

Recommendation for Benjamin Flock

It is a great pleasure to provide this letter of recommendation for Benjamin Flock. I have known Ben since he was a tenth grader at Green Pastures High School. Always a dynamic force in his class and a strong positive role model for other students, Ben is well respected and loved by staff and students alike.

I got to know Ben very well during our training workshops for a peer mediation team that was established at our school. During those workshops Ben exhibited unusual maturity for a young man his age. He consistently demonstrated warmth, kindness and sincerity. He embodies those necessary inherent skills that ensures his success as a "helping professional."

Skills he developed in training involved learning impartiality, teaching others how to listen to an opposing view, taking in emotionally charged information while remaining calm, and summarizing the positions of those being mediated so both parties could feel fully and accurately represented. He learned what types of information called for "private sessions" and how to integrate (with the party's permission) or keep separate what was learned in a private session. Because our mediators worked in teams of two, I was also happy to see Ben easily work with all partners he was assigned. He was equally comfortable with females, younger students and those with whom he did not share common interests.

I was truly impressed with Ben after the training workshops were over and peer mediations began to take place in our school. While some of the trainees were not confident enough to respond on a moment's notice, Ben always made himself available for an emergency mediation, sometimes sacrificing his own needs. He also could be counted on to take care of his personal responsibilities and class work when called out of class unexpectedly.

I heartily recommend Ben for any position that involves the care of others. He would be an excellent resident advisor. He has the skills and humanity to protect others and lead them in a positive direction.

Sincerely,

"He consistently demonstrated warmth, kindness and sincerity. He embodies those necessary inherent skills that ensures his success as a helping professional."

Recommendation for Carl Young

I am happy to offer this letter of recommendation on behalf of Carl Young. I have known Carl for three years as the advisor for the peer mediators.

Carl has had a very rough childhood. For this reason, the person whose application you are now considering is a *success story*. Carl was abandoned by his father and had to care for his sister alone in an apartment before he was ten. They had been starving— living under the worst possible conditions. When Carl returned to his mother in Indiana, he was able to pick himself up and carry on.

Carl has pursued a series of rigorous courses, including those chosen for his senior year. He excels in sports, but also in music where he is one of the most accomplished musicians to develop at our high school. He also has won top awards for acting ability in our school plays. Carl has not shied away from hard science or math, and he has completed four years of Latin. He is highly respected by teachers and students.

"He is a natural; mature, poised and respectful to others. People trust him. I feel he has a high degree of empathy and great "people skills" because of his difficult childhood."

Recently, Carl and I have worked together to mediate peer disputes. He had volunteered to undergo intensive training to become skilled in this method of problem solving. He is a natural; mature, poised and respectful to others. People trust him. I feel he has a high degree of empathy and great "people skills" *because* of his difficult childhood.

I have full confidence that Carl can handle any position in public relations that he undertakes, and further, will make many valuable contributions to your place of employment.

Sincerely,

Mature Beyond Their Years

Recommendation for Jonas Chalk

Jonas Chalk is a fine young man. He is a serious student and contributes substantially to his classes. He is an all-star football player, but remains focused on academics. Jonas is polite, well-groomed and well-liked by teachers and students alike.

Jonas is a great writer. He is also conscientious about responsibilities, has an old-fashioned work ethic and is open to learning from others. Jonas's intelligence is tempered with kindness and grace. Though a physically imposing young man, he is thoughtful, modest and considerate.

Jonas has been raised since birth by his aunt and uncle. They are people of simple means. Any assistance you can offer in the form of a scholarship will go a long way to helping Jonas to reach his goals.

Sincerely,

"He is also conscientious about responsibilities, has an old-fashioned work ethic and is open to learning from others. Jonas's intelligence is tempered with kindness and grace."

Mature Beyond Their Years

Recommendation for Walter Bombright

Walter Bombright is an extremely mature young man whose focus is strongly academic. He is a late bloomer who experienced a period of emotional turmoil while away at boarding school. He returned to the public school system as a junior and has exhibited tremendous self-control, seriousness of purpose and self-awareness.

Walter has given of himself in many extracurricular activities on the field and behind the scenes. His adjustment to his new school has been smooth and he has made many new friends in a short amount of time. He is well liked by students and faculty alike. I have seen an enormous growth in the last year and a half, and I have the utmost confidence in his ability to excel at Euphoria College. He will be an excellent role model for others.

Please feel free to contact me if you would like further information about Walter. I am happy to recommend him to your college.

Sincerely,

"Walter has exhibited tremendous self-control, seriousness of purpose and self-awareness... (he) has given of himself in many extracurricular activities on the field and behind the scenes. His adjustment to his new school has been smooth and he has made many new friends in a short amount of time."

Movers and Shakers

Recommendation for Gloria Mienmen

I am delighted to write this recommendation on behalf of Gloria Mienmen. I have known Gloria for three years as her guidance counselor.

Gloria is a gifted student and a strong, extremely mature individual. Gloria has tremendous depth, sense of purpose and drive, and is broad-minded. She has excelled here and augmented her schooling with many courses at the local college. Her talents range from the fine arts (painting, drawing, sculpting, classical guitar) to advanced science (Physics at the college level), yet she has always had time for athletics.

Gloria has taken a leadership role at school as president of the National Honor Society for two years, as student advisory council member, and as a student representative to our school policy committee.

Gloria loves art. She loves science. She is a determined athlete. She has won many medals, ribbons and letters in various sports. Gloria is happiest when she is learning something new, taking a difficult course, moving beyond the limits of her experience. Her priorities are on the development of her character and her talents. She is unswayed by the superficial pressures of her generation, is self-directed and self-possessed. Gloria is also a loyal friend and an extremely sensitive person.

"Gloria loves art. She loves science. She is a determined athlete... has won many medals, ribbons and letters in various sports... is happiest when she is learning something new, taking a difficult course, moving beyond the limits of her experience."

Gloria is an independent thinker and spirit. She follows her own strong volitions without concern for what others may think. This enables her to have tremendous freedom and to be happy and confident. Her inner voice is strong. This quality is also the source for her creative energy.

Gloria is sensitive to others. As a volunteer on our staff of students working to incorporate diversity into our school, Gloria worked with faculty and students to find strategies to help broaden the awareness of issues of diversity. The efforts of this group of students enabled us to create a safer school environment.

Gloria continues to challenge herself in her selection of courses for her senior year. Her essential quality is that of a lifelong student. I know she will make a great contribution in whatever field she chooses and will incorporate her many talents in this effort. Without hesitation, I give Gloria my highest recommendation.

Sincerely,

Recommendation for Susan T. Lanthoney

I am delighted to offer this letter of recommendation on behalf of Susan Lanthoney. I have known Susan for three years as advisor to the Women's Studies Club. She is one of the students I know very well from this group, and it is my honor to be acquainted with her.

Susan has a rich and unique character. In many ways, she is both an old fashioned girl and a Renaissance woman. Susan has a heightened awareness of women's issues. This awareness has grown as a result of her personal experiences as an avid golfer, as the only girl on our envirothon team, and her courage to be different from other girls over the years.

She is a strong, confident young person.

Susan provided me with many resources for a class I taught last year on gender equity issues, though not taking the class herself. She also attended the Women's Conference through Mobern College in order to broaden her awareness of these issues and meet with people from diverse backgrounds.

Susan continues in hard sciences and math, excels in social studies and English, and challenges herself in foreign language. She began her studies in Latin for "fun" as a junior.

Susan does not follow the whims of style, but creates her own. She is not shy about her talents, but she gives life to them. She is a role model for others, teaching by example how one might live one's life as an independent person. She is a woman on the move; she does not look back.

"Susan does not follow the whims of style, but creates her own. She is not shy about her talents, but gives life to them... a role model for others, teaches by example how one might live one's life as an independent person. She is a woman on the move."

Susan has a truly original spirit and has a talent for the arts in many forms (dance, crafts). She is a gardener, a landscaper, naturalist, athlete, furniture refinisher, car mechanic (she rebuilt an old Corvette—body and engine—for three years—which she drives now), as well as having a variety of academic gifts.

A quick look at Susan's GPA or SAT may belie my contention that she is extremely talented academically. I believe one contributing factor for this has been that Susan has been dealing with the sudden loss of her mother at the start of her freshman year in a tragic accident. Susan has had to grow up quickly, to deal with intense grief and to take on new roles at home all at once. My impression is that she has done so and has not lost her own identity while helping care for the rest of her family. She has held onto her *self* in the face of this storm, and I greatly admire her for it. She will do ground breaking things in the future. Should you accept her into your program, you will have a leader, a wise, fun and talented person, and I believe she will enrich your student body and your faculty.

Sincerely,

Recommendation for Richard Starklee

I am happy to offer this recommendation on behalf of Richard Starklee. I have known Richard for three years.

Richard is *so* full of life. He exudes energy. He is the kind of person whose presence reminds me to live in the moment. Richard has tremendous enthusiasm and energy for all that he does.

Richard excels at foreign languages, in social science and English studies. He also has a terrific ability to perform on stage. He is respected by faculty and students because of his outgoing and cheerful personality, as well as his excellence in classroom participation where he has a depth of understanding that belies his age. Both his English teachers and social studies teachers over the years have valued his contributions tremendously.

"(Richard is)... respected by faculty and students because of his outgoing and cheerful personality, as well as his excellence in classroom participation where he has a depth of understanding that belies his age."

I consider Richard a great all around talent. I am confident that when he is able to explore all the possibilities available to him after high school, he is going to blossom into an even more outstanding human being.

I know that Richard will be successful in any program he chooses to explore. I wholeheartedly recommend him to your technical school. He will not only prove himself in academics, but in many extracurricular areas as well.

Sincerely,

Movers and Shakers

Recommendation for Bella Arnez

Bella Arnez stands alone. She is an individual—strong and freethinking; her eyes are brilliant and flashing from depths waiting to be fully explored. Never looking back or taking a sideward glance to her peers, setting the direction by her own inner guide and adventurous spirit, she leads by example the others who watch her. Her courage and uniqueness awe them.

Bella is a loyal friend, wise in many ways, yet also resembling a "diamond in the rough." When the edges get a bit sharp, I have found her to take direction well, reflecting on better methods of reaching her goals and also maintaining the support of others.

The myriad ways she has extended herself through activities at school is truly impressive. Bella is an artist, a thinker, challenging with confidence what appears before her. She has made strides to *establish* the clubs and activities that have created opportunities for many others to learn and share in ways not possible during the typical school day. A founder of our Women's Studies Club, a supporter of our Gay-Straight Alliance, President of Amnesty International and Vice President to the National Art Honor Society for two years, she gives generously of her time. Seeing her perform her freshman speech to a packed and silenced auditorium of parents and peers was an experience of a lifetime for me. Bella gave fifteen minutes of a well-known soliloquy with passion and humor. This set her apart in the fall of her first year with us. Easily winning first place, her performance has not been equaled since.

Bella also sets standards for excellence in the classroom. Equally gifted in verbal and mathematical areas, shining as well in our most difficult science courses, Bella can go in any direction her heart desires. She will pave the road for new thinking in academics as well as the arts. Should Bella be accepted to your institution for this fall, I am confident she will add enormously to student culture in and outside the classroom. My recommendation is without reservation.

Sincerely,

"The myriad ways she has extended herself through activities at school is truly impressive. Bella is an artist, a thinker, challenging with confidence what appears before her. She has made strides to establish the clubs and activities that have created opportunities for many others...."

Recommendation for Jane Frawley

I have known Jane Frawley for three years as her club advisor for the school newspaper. Jane is an extremely enthusiastic young woman who has tremendous energy. She approaches all she does with a strong desire to do well.

Jane has been involved in numerous activities, but I know her best for her work with our school newspaper. She is energized by researching current affairs and contemporary issues, and is courageous when reporting on controversial topics. Jane's spirit seems to have a life of its own when it comes to investigative reporting and follow through. Even under pressure to meet deadlines, she has fulfilled all commitments undertaken with a positive, buoyant spirit.

"Jane's spirit seems to have a life of its own when it comes to investigative reporting and follow through. Even under pressure to meet deadlines, she has fulfilled all commitments undertaken with a positive, buoyant spirit."

Jane also is a talented actress, very much involved in a variety of school activities. She has devoted herself to learning about and educating others to community and global issues.

I have found Jane to be extremely personable, mature, full of life and generous with her time. All indicators are there for her to grow into a very successful woman in any area she wishes to pursue. You will find her a bright and lively addition to the editorial staff of your paper.

Sincerely,

Recommendation for Constance Hong

I am pleased to offer this letter for a scholarship award on behalf of Constance Hong. I have known Connie for three years as her guidance counselor and as the advisor for the school newspaper that she edits.

Connie has grown tremendously in maturity over the past three years. She has become focused, confident and capable. Academically, she has tackled challenging subjects and done well. In her extracurricular activities, Connie is devoted and she consistently puts her "all" into many clubs. She created new directions for our chapter of SADD, is involved in student government, and gives her time and energy to her class activities.

"Connie takes on many writing assignments for the paper on short notice and still meets deadlines without a complaint. Connie also devotes many hours working with teachers, administrators and community representatives on various advisory councils within our school."

A constant contributor to our school newspaper, she has served as editor of current events issues for three years. What always impresses me is that Connie takes on many writing assignments for the paper on short notice and still meets deadlines without a complaint. Connie also devotes many hours working with teachers, administrators and community representatives on various advisory councils within our school.

In addition to the time Connie spends with school activities, she has held a job outside of school for the past three years. The experiences she has had in the world of work have greatly added to her confidence, enabling her to bring to fruit some of the gifts she will no doubt demonstrate in the years to come.

I have the utmost confidence that Connie will make great contributions to the world as she continues to grow. She is a real "go-getter," courageous and devoted to helping others with the gifts she possesses.

Sincerely,

Just Some
Great All Around Kids

Recommendation for Margaret Weed

I am very happy to offer this letter of recommendation for Margaret Weed. She is a hard working young woman, mature, poised and kind. A quiet person, a person of depth and perseverance, she has challenged some of our most difficult courses without complaint and done extremely well.

Margaret has continued in her Latin classes throughout her career here, continued in math (although she has long since fulfilled her graduation requirements), and (similarly) continued in the sciences. Her true devotion at this time is the arts, and she tackles these courses with the same sense of earnestness as the others. She works to expand her mind and her life.

Well traveled, having lived all over the world, Margaret's maturity comes from a wide range of experiences. She brings much to classroom discussions and her writing. I know this talent will blossom in the areas she has yet to explore.

I am happy to highly recommend Margaret to your technical program.

Sincerely,

"Well traveled, having lived all over the world, Margaret's maturity comes from a wide range of experiences. She brings much to classroom discussions and her writing."

Recommendation for Jacqueline Boyner

Jacqueline Boyner is dynamic, mature, funny—a very bright young woman. She is creative, confident, outgoing and sensitive.

Jackie has always challenged herself in the most difficult courses we offer. I believe this is because she has a natural curiosity and energy for life. She wants to learn in order to satisfy her own inner nature to explore the world. This is a rare quality.

Jackie is very well liked amongst peers, teachers and administrators. Earning the trust of peers, she has been elected captain of our field hockey team this year. When she was a sophomore, we worked together on our school literary magazine. She was the Sports Editor, a daunting task for a tenth grader. She fulfilled her responsibilities with joy, humor and innovation. This is no easy role to fulfill, especially because Jackie has many other commitments, however, she made all deadlines and added needed spunk to the publication.

I will miss Jackie next year. She is one of the few students who relate to adults with confidence, courtesy and openness. She will add to campus life in a very positive way, and I am confident she will succeed in all her endeavors. She is a winner.

Sincerely,

"She was the Sports Editor (for the school paper)... and has fulfilled her responsibilities with joy, humor and innovation."

Just Some
Great All Around Kids

Recommendation for Christine Crinkley

I am delighted to offer this letter on behalf of Christine Crinkley, whom I have known for three years as her counselor at Glad View High School.

Chrissie is so bright, so full of energy and so positive in her outlook that it can be contagious. This disposition is based on a solid foundation of spirit and intellect. Considering her record over the years, this is clear. This year she chose the most difficult courses we have to offer and is performing well.

Chrissie is as comfortable cheering on the squad as she is being the only girl in her electronics class of twenty-one students. When I asked her how she felt in that situation, she said it never really occurred to her that she was outnumbered!

"Lots of young women have academic talent, not all are as well rounded, as down to earth, as embracing ...(she will be) the type of doctor that I would want to take care of me if I become ill—humanistic, a great listener, someone with deep concern."

Chrissie is so hard working and determined that she seems to handle any course, even those of the utmost difficulty, with excellence. Lots of young women have academic talent, not all are as well rounded, as down to earth and as embracing to others as Chrissie. I can envision her being the type of doctor that I would want to take care of me if I become ill—humanistic, a great listener, someone with deep concern.

I am an alum of Studyall University, where I earned my degree in Counseling Psychology. I can definitely see Chrissie not only fitting into your campus student population, but taking on leadership roles, encouraging others, enlivening the entire atmosphere of her dorm, her classes, her activities. I recommend her without reservation.

Sincerely,

Capable Students Who Stay Behind the Scenes

Capable Students Who Stay Behind the Scenes

Recommendation for Andrew Adams

I am very happy to offer this letter of recommendation on behalf of Andrew Adams. I have known Andy for three years as his guidance counselor.

Andy has developed incredibly over these past three years. The experience he had hosting an exchange student for a year was life-altering for him. As you will read in his essay, living with a Spanish family in Madrid further matured him. Andy has a strong confidence in himself that rests just below a healthy dose of humility. This, I feel, is a great combination of characteristics in a human being.

Newly discovered talents in Photography and Computer Programming classes have enabled Andy to find success and to take risks. From this he has reaped recognition and many other intangible rewards. The combination of experiences mentioned here is, I believe, important contributing factors to the dramatic increase in Andy's self-assurance and self-esteem.

"A hard worker, Andy has chosen courses of substance and depth over the years. A variety of extracurricular activities have also rounded him as a person. I was impressed by the response he gave..."

A hard worker, Andy has chosen courses of substance and depth over the years. A variety of extracurricular activities also have rounded him as a person. I was impressed by the response he gave when I asked him to become the staff photographer for the school literary magazine (that I oversee). He jumped at the chance and followed through with every meeting and assignment. When caught without his camera one day, he went to a great deal of trouble to go home to get one so that he might take the necessary photographs. Although I asked him not to bother, he insisted and was happy to exert himself to take care of the task at hand. I really appreciated that extra effort and admired his positive attitude.

Andy is a solid student, very likable and a great team player. He will excel in a college environment and add much to campus activities as well. I recommend him without reservation.

Sincerely,

Capable Students Who Stay Behind the Scenes

Recommendation for Elizabeth Blackspell

I am writing on behalf of Elizabeth Blackspell, whom I have known for three years as her guidance counselor. Betsy is a kind, genuine, bright young woman. She is a very hard worker, a student who has always challenged herself. Each year, Betsy has chosen a steady core of challenging courses and worked diligently. She continued her Latin through four years, her science through Advanced Biology, and most significantly, her math, not her best subject, nor one she has avoided. I really admire her attitude to press on though difficulty and not seek the easy way.

Betsy has taken on a leadership role as captain of our girls' basketball team. She has been active in school plays, preparing floats for homecoming events each year and working closely with a student with multiple handicaps in a program at our school for severely handicapped children. The child Betsy works with has multiple disabilities, as you will read in her essay. Most would shy away from the kind of challenge this child presents, but not Betsy. She is perfectly suited for a career in health services. If I were the patient, I'd feel secure in her care. She is an embracing person, non-judgmental, with high ethical standards.

Betsy has tremendous depth to her character. She epitomizes the phrase "still waters run deep," for within her quietness lies a great person, the kind of person anyone would want for a friend.

I heartily recommend Elizabeth Blackspell to your nursing program.

> Sincerely,

"She is perfectly suited for a career in health services. If I were the patient, I'd feel secure in her care. She is an embracing person, non-judgmental, with high ethical standards."

Capable Students Who Stay Behind the Scenes

Recommendation for Peter Lemming

I have known Peter Lemming for three years as his history teacher. What impresses me most about Peter is his confidence, sincerity, energy and resiliency.

Academically, Peter is very talented and a diligent worker. He has always elected to take the most challenging courses our school has to offer and has excelled. He is a valued member of our soccer team, as well as our school band. He has held down an after school job each year throughout high school, and he still managed to perform at the top of his class. This year he has been team teaching art classes to sixth graders twice monthly after school.

Peter was one of the only young men in the school who had the independence of spirit to take a women's history class. There he participated with more sincerity and effort than any other student. Each report, whether written or oral, was done extremely well; his ability to debate and engage in dialogue was strong.

"Peter was one of the only young men in the school who had the independence of spirit to take a women's history class. There he participated with more sincerity and effort than any other student."

Most impressive is Peter's ability to self-reflect and consider others' points of view, and then to reshape his own thinking based on this reflection. He worked equally well with ninth graders who were less verbal and seniors (while a junior) who held strong, steadfast opinions. In fact, his points of view often functioned as an anchor on choppy seas as he demonstrated a deep and broad knowledge of social issues and a command of history.

Peter is extremely friendly, mature, well-mannered, genuine, and he has tremendous depth of character. He has been a strong example of moral integrity to his friends, teammates and classmates. Last year, Peter was a witness to the harassment of students when traveling with a team on the school bus. Distressed by their behavior, he was able to take action to change the situation. Peter Lemming demonstrates qualities natural to a leader: sensitivity, independence, open mindedness, conviction and courage.

Peter will excel in any chosen area at college. I recommend him without reservation.

Sincerely,

Capable Students Who Stay Behind the Scenes

Letter of Recommendation for James Jimenez

I am happy to write this letter on behalf of James Jimenez. He is a serious student who has worked hard for his grades and class standing and not shied away from difficult courses. His deep interest lies in physical therapy. His record in the sciences and math show that he is a "plugger." Never taking an easy route, he knows how to work hard and apply himself to the challenges before him in order to attain his goals. He is a solid, disciplined student.

Jimmy also has proven himself a well-rounded young man. He has earned the trust of teammates in soccer and baseball, and has captained both teams this year. He has been elected to student council for two years, and been a member of our National Honor Society. He has also extended himself in various clubs throughout his high school career.

Recently, Jimmy embarked on a community improvement project to substantially brighten and refurbish our local town park. He has solicited supplies from local businesses, encouraged other students to work on the project and managed the organization of all details.

I have total confidence that Jimmy will succeed in college in his chosen field and will give of himself in the college setting as he has at Green Pastures High School. He is very a deserving candidate for the Good Samaritan Award Scholarship.

Sincerely,

"Never taking an easy route, he knows how to work hard and apply himself to the challenges before him in order to make his goals. He is a solid, disciplined student."

Recommendation for Marilyn Alright

Marilyn Alright is one of the hardest working students I have known. She never shies away from challenges—personal or academic. I see her consistently plugging away through difficult courses and dealing with difficult situations maturely.

Marilyn has never taken the easy way out. As I look over her transcript for the past four years, I see that she has chosen courses that other students avoided. Marilyn has taken the better route—seeking out teachers for extra help and always trying her best. I have also witnessed Marilyn's composure, self-confidence and maturity during some difficult times. She handles herself well.

"...she has chosen courses that other students avoided. Marilyn has taken the better route—seeking out teachers for extra help and always trying her best."

Marilyn is focused, task oriented and gets things done. She is self-motivated, kind, sensitive and reflective. She is a loyal friend, a cheerful companion. In her own quiet way, she makes great contributions in all endeavors. I recommend her to your company with enthusiasm. She will be an excellent employee.

Sincerely,

Academic Achievers

Recommendation for Rolph Bader

I am pleased to offer this recommendation for Rolph Bader. I have been his guidance counselor for three years. During this time I have watched Rolph express his tremendous potential. This young man is gifted in many areas, so much so that I am awed by his contrasting humble, modest demeanor.

As you can see from his transcript, Rolph has taken the most challenging courses we have to offer and won top awards for academic excellence. He has excelled at athletics and been a respected leader of his teammates.

"Rolph... adds insight to (class) discussions, he participates enthusiastically, is creative and extremely conscientious."

Rolph is also friendly and outgoing and is extremely well liked by his classmates. Teachers enjoy having Rolph in class because he adds insight to discussions, he participates enthusiastically, is creative and *extremely* conscientious. Rolph is also respectful and sensitive to others. He has excellent character.

Rolph has devoted himself to numerous community activities and undertakes everything with great seriousness. He supports others, reaches out and values those around him.

Part of the blend of all the qualities I have mentioned is deep, quiet strength and self-confidence. Rolph's presence is unassuming, understated. He is polite—a gentleman. I have the utmost confidence that he will be successful at anything he undertakes.

Sincerely,

Recommendation for Barbara Salter

Barbara Salter is a gifted scholar—a serious student with a wide range of talents. Her record speaks for itself. She is also involved in numerous school activities and in the larger community. She is a great role model and an active participant in all her chosen areas.

What impresses our staff above all is Barbara's consistent ability to work hard, produce quality work, lead by example and be involved in a great variety of groups that take considerable extra time. She is a team player and can work within groups. Refreshingly, she is not overbearing although she is tremendously talented. Barbara never seems to be overextending herself. She is modest (though not self-effacing), and has many deep, lifelong friendships.

"She is a team player and can work within groups. Refreshingly, she is not overbearing although she is tremendously talented."

Barbara has much to offer and I am confident that she will find her own ways to enhance student culture and classroom standards next year. If accepted to your school, you will find your school also enriched by her brilliance, sense of commitment, spirit and compassion for others.

Sincerely,

Academic Achievers

Recommendation for Christopher Tryden

I have known Christopher Tryden for three years. It is a pleasure to offer this letter of recommendation on his behalf. As his guidance counselor, I have worked with Chris to create the most challenging schedule each year for this talented young man. I have also gotten to know Chris more informally through the daily comings and goings of students at our small school.

Chris stands out as our top-ranking senior academically, however, he also has so much more to his credit. Chris is talented in sports, as a leader and as a school citizen. He is well mannered, wholesome, quiet and calm. He maintains his composure under pressure, yet also has a sense of humor and a strong sense of responsibility.

A sense of responsibility is one of his most enduring qualities. Chris has worked each summer for four years at the Family Factory, learning the value of cooperation, of relationships and what it takes to create a business and to keep it growing. As a class officer during his junior year, the story is well known that when their house was totally flooded during the night, Chris had the presence of mind to grab up the class records and paperwork before making an escape. Then, he went to school the next day!

A respected member of the basketball team, Chris has become a team player over the years—a skill I know will help him face the challenges to come. His verbal skills are extremely sharp, as are his research abilities. He has taken on many new experiences on our debate team that have helped him develop and demonstrate the depth of knowledge he has and his ability to communicate.

"His verbal skills are extremely sharp, as are his research abilities. He has taken on many new experiences on our debate team that have helped him develop and demonstrate the depth of knowledge he has and his ability to communicate."

As vice president of the National Honor Society, Chris has volunteered his time to organize a peer tutoring program that enables many students to have needed academic support from other students. In addition, Chris has always taken the most demanding classes our school has to offer, and will be taking a college course in computers at a local college this spring.

Chris is an eager learner and, though gifted, has a quiet humility. He has developed a strong confidence from within, because of what he has *accomplished,* rather than because of the recognition he has received. I consider him a great all-around person, very likable, someone whose talents and character will be an asset to your school and to your student body.

Sincerely,

Recommendation for Louise Rae Balmott

Louise Rae Balmott has been a student of mine for over two years. She is a gifted young woman with a deep and mature nature, who has persevered through very difficult personal circumstances.

I met Louise when she was a sophomore, adjusting to her father's death. This was a sudden and shocking event. I expected her grades to suffer, but instead she remained steadfast in her efforts to do well. I really admire her for this.

Louise has taken the most challenging courses that our school offers throughout her four years here, and this year has gone a step further. She is one of the few seniors who is taking advantage of a new program that our state is offering whereby students can earn college credit and high school credit simultaneously by attending our local state university. Louise is currently enrolled at our local state college for Psychology and Graphic Arts.

"Louise Rae is talented artistically as well as academically. She has been a member of the National Art Honor Society. She has done beautiful work and has helped to create stunning murals for our school corridors."

Louise is talented artistically as well as academically. She has been a member of the National Art Honor Society. She has done beautiful work and has helped to create stunning murals for our school corridors.

In addition to excelling at school, Louise has been an equestrian for many years. She has taken responsibility for the money required to support this interest. Louise also has taken on a leadership role at the local horse stables. She has been responsible for the care and training of the horses and for educating newer members of the group. When involved in a competition as captain of the club, Louise must engage in formal dialogue with judges when the scores of teammates are disputed and she must represent her teammates at "hearings." In these situations, this often quiet person displays confidence under pressure, independence, logic, reason and courage.

I am confident that Louise will continue to blossom as a student on your campus. Please feel free to contact me for further information.

Sincerely,

Recommendation for John Sousa

John Sousa is an exceptional student; this you can easily tell from looking at his transcript. What the official record does not tell you is that John is mature, responsible, thoughtful and has tremendous concern for others.

John has devoted himself to coaching elementary school children. One day it rained; practice for the children was cancelled. John, then a junior, kept all the children with him while he phoned their homes and arranged rides for the team.

Memorial Day 20XX. Our school band was slated to play in our traditional ceremony on the front lawn. The band's conductor was called away in an emergency. Who became the ad hoc conductor on short notice? John Sousa of course. Capable, well liked, working well under pressure. *Supportive.*

We trust John. He is gifted academically, yet he is so much more. He is liked and respected by peers and faculty. I am confident that he will add a special dimension to classroom discussion and to campus life as well.

Sincerely,

"He is gifted academically, yet he is so much more. He is liked and respected by peers and faculty. I am confident that he will add a special dimension to classroom discussion and to campus life as well."

Recommendation for Elizabeth Crolle

I am happy to offer this letter of recommendation on behalf of Elizabeth Crolle. I have known Beth for three years as her guidance counselor.

I like Beth. She is calm, centered, with a good head on her shoulders. She has not bent to the whims or fads of her generation, but is clearly her own person. She has numerous interests, has participated faithfully in basketball each year and has been involved in many other clubs and service organizations within the school.

Beth has been elected to the student council each year. She is now its president. This demonstrates the respect her peers have for her. Our faculty feels the same way. I have found her to be forthright, confident and considerate.

Beth will excel at college. I attended a breakfast meeting with one of your representatives last fall. I learned a great deal about your school, saw beautiful photographs and learned the essence of campus life. I feel that Beth would fit in well. She is wholesome, honest, trustworthy and a friend to others. She has much to contribute to a school community. I know she will thrive at college. I recommend her without reservation.

Sincerely,

"I learned a great deal about your school... and learned the essence of its campus culture. I feel that Beth would fit in well. She is wholesome, honest, trustworthy and a friend to others."

Recommendation for Jane Woodwall

I am delighted to offer this letter of recommendation on behalf of Jane Woodwall. Jane is an extremely talented young woman with a broad range of interests, whom I consider to be one of the best this generation has to offer the future.

Jane is very highly regarded by the faculty for her excellence in academics. She displays unusual gifts in art and language as well. Quiet and reserved by nature, Jane tried something different when she came to the high school. Basketball at the junior varsity and then varsity level, and her role as co-captain of the team this year, has clearly enabled her to discover more about her potential, so that her manner is now easy, confident and assured.

Jane is a member of our National Honor Society. For two years she has graciously provided tutoring as needed to our students. She is gifted academically and also has patience and compassion for others. As an officer of the National Art Honor Society, Jane has grown further. She also has been a member of the Environmental Science team that meets each morning to prepare for competition.

"Jane has innate gifts, but I've been pleased to watch her over time as she has taken more risks, as she did during a foreign exchange experience she had in Spain last year, and to orchestrate the front page article for our school paper about the trip."

Jane has innate gifts, but I've been pleased to watch her over time as she has taken more risks, as she did during a foreign exchange experience she had in Spain last year, and to orchestrate the front page article for our school paper about the trip.

Jane will excel at college. I am confident that any program of studies she pursues will enable her to further grow and to make significant contributions to the world before her.

Sincerely,

Recommendation for Henry Messenger

Henry Messenger is a kind person. He is rich in humanitarian values. His combination of intellectual gifts and his sense of responsibility for others enables one to see what the true value of intelligence and sensitivity can bring to the world.

Henry has never held back. He engages in a variety of community activities, and though serious, is comfortable at play in theatrical roles as well as in sports. He has not shied away from the painstaking work of our school's Handbook Committee, where, representing students, he could influence the faculty, staff, parents and administrators as school policy matters were negotiated. This takes a depth and confidence that is rare in students at this level, yet Henry dedicated many weeks after school to complete the task.

Henry is a talented student, a loyal friend, the "all around" person whose presence enhances any arena. I recommend him enthusiastically.

Sincerely,

"His combination of intellectual gifts and his sense of responsibility for others enables one to see what the true value of intelligence and sensitivity can bring to the world."

Recommendation for Robert Fischler

Robert Fischler is an excellent student and an exceptional young man. I have known Robert for three years and have helped him to schedule his classes each year. He has always exerted himself to take the most demanding subjects we have to offer.

Robert is so bright, so capable in every area—verbal, mathematical and scientific—that it is impossible to indicate a special ability. He is also a great team player and has been involved in many sports each year, e.g., Varsity Soccer, Track, Varsity Basketball. He is a member of the National Honor Society, has participated in class plays each year, is a member of Students Against Drunk Driving, the Youth in Government Club and the Chess Club. He also represented our school last year at a national youth in government event.

Robert comes from a wonderful family. He is second of six children. His parents always have placed a high value on education. Their careful parenting has enabled him to become extremely articulate and well-mannered. Teachers love having Robert in class, not only because of his intelligence, but because of his insight and participation in class discussions.

I have full confidence that Robert will succeed beautifully in any endeavor he undertakes. I recommend him enthusiastically.

Sincerely,

"Robert is so bright, so capable in every area—verbal, mathematical and scientific—that it is impossible to indicate a special ability."

Sometimes the words don't come, the images of the student in the past and the future don't spark anything, and you still need to conjure up a letter. Also, at times, you feel the best of the student has yet to be realized. You don't want to refuse to write a letter because a) it would insult the student and b) he or she does need a recommendation. You also want to be true to yourself, not inflating the student's good qualities. You want to tell the truth.

It may be hard to be totally frank. My advice—increase the font size and be pleasantly vague. The reader should be able to read between the lines. This section includes some examples of this method of creative writing.

The Hardest Ones to Write

The Hardest Ones to Write

Recommendation for Joseph Sough

Joseph Sough has devoted himself to service for others during his four years at Green Pastures High School. He consistently has represented his class as its president for three years. He has reached out to create new activities here at school, bringing diversity workshops to students and attending leadership conferences on behalf of his class.

Joseph is enthusiastic, bright, energetic and positive. I am sure he will advance even further as the years go on.

Sincerely,

"He has reached out to create new activities here at school, bringing diversity workshops to students and attending leadership conferences on behalf of his class."

Recommendation for Eric Grafton

Eric Grafton is a very wholesome, well-mannered young man. He has a wonderful set of personal values and deep humility. He also is talented academically. He will excel in the field of engineering because he has the abilities to focus and to take his work very seriously.

Eric also has good self-discipline and works well in a team. He is respected by staff and peers alike. He has a "never give up" spirit. He continually challenges himself on our track teams as well as in his choice of courses each year. I recommend Eric Grafton without reservation.

Sincerely,

"Eric Grafton is a very wholesome, well-mannered young man. He has a wonderful set of personal values and deep humility."

Recommendation for Barbara Kwan

I am happy to offer this letter of recommendation on behalf of Barbara Kwan. She has been a student at Green Acres High School for four years; I have known her for three as her guidance counselor.

Barbara has done very well academically. She is a hard worker, has a positive outlook and participates enthusiastically in all of her classes. An active learner, I know Barbara will put tremendous effort into her college education as she has done here. I am confident that the next chapter of Barbara's life will enable her to realize even more of her potential as she pursues her interests at college.

I have visited your campus, as has Barbara, and we feel this environment will be an excellent match for her. Please feel free to call me with any questions you may have about her prospective candidacy.

Sincerely,

"I am confident that the next chapter of Barbara's life will enable her to realize even more of her potential as she pursues her interests at college."

Recommendation for Marc Ragall

Marc Ragall is a very mature young man with a deep sense of purpose. He is sensitive to others, a great team player and is well respected among peers and faculty.

Marc works at his studies. He is thoughtful and focused. I know him to be self-motivated and inner directed—qualities that ensure he will make the most of his educational opportunities.

Marc has always been interested in the Fine Arts. Because of his sincerity, I know he will be an excellent student. He is eager to learn—eager to gain skills to pursue his dream. I think the world of Marc, and know he will be successful in his endeavors. Please feel free if you would like to discuss his candidacy in more detail.

Sincerely,

"He is thoughtful and focused. I know him to be self-motivated and inner directed—qualities that ensure he will make the most of his educational opportunities."

Recommendation for Steven Marteen

I have known Steven Marteen for four years. He is a quiet, modest young man who has a serious attitude toward life. He is likable and focused.

Steven is looking forward to succeeding in college. He will need to further develop the qualities mentioned, and, because he is capable of doing fine work, it will be necessary for him to extend his serious attitude into the effort he applies to his studies. I am confident that Steven will do his best to rise to the occasion.

Sincerely,

"... because he is capable of doing fine work, it will be necessary for him to extend his serious attitude into the effort he applies to his studies."

Descriptive Words and Phrases

A

able
active
admirable
adventurous spirit
ample reservoir of expertise
asset in the classroom

B

best is yet to come
bright
brilliant
broad-minded
buoyant spirit

C

calm
calm under pressure
change-agent
committed to developing self
compassionate
conscientious
considerate
courageous
creative

D

depth
determined
devoted
diligent
dynamic
dynamic spirit

E

eager learner
earnest
ebullient spirit
embracing
energized
enormous energy
enthusiastic

Add your own favorites here

_____
_____
_____
_____
_____

_____
_____
_____
_____

_____
_____
_____
_____
_____
_____
_____
_____
_____

_____
_____
_____
_____
_____

_____
_____
_____
_____
_____
_____

E (cont.)

excellent character

exceptional young woman

exerted self

expansive

exudes confidence

F

focused

follows through

forthright

forward-looking

freethinking

friend to others

friendly

full of life

funny

G

generous with time

genuine

gifted

go-getter

good head on shoulders

great listener

H

high ethical standards

high-energy

highly motivated

honest

humanistic

humble

I

I admire her (him)

I like him (her)

incredible human being

independent

inner reserve

innovative

insightful

inspires others

integrity

I (cont.)

intelligent _____

invested in own growth _____

involved _____

K

kind _____

kindhearted _____

L

leads by example _____

lifelong student _____

lively _____

loyal _____

M

mature _____

modest _____

much to contribute _____

N

natural leader _____

non-judgmental _____

not swayed by others _____

nothing stops her _____

O

old-fashioned work ethic _____

one-of-a-kind _____

optimistic _____

outgoing _____

outstanding verbal skills _____

own person _____

P

perseverance _____

person of grace and perseverance _____

personable _____

plugger _____

poised _____

positive _____

positive attitude _____

positive influence _____

possesses a quiet intelligence _____

Q

quiet _____

quiet confidence _____

quiet strength _____

quintessential student _____

R

radiant _____

radiates enthusiasm _____

reaches out _____

reliable _____

S

self-directed _____

self-assured _____

self-confident _____

self-effacing _____

self-possessed _____

self-sufficient _____

selfless _____

sense of commitment _____

sense of purpose _____

sensitive _____

serious _____

sets standards for excellence _____

sincere _____

skilled _____

spunky _____

stands alone _____

strict with self _____

strong confidence _____

strong inner voice _____

strong sense of responsibility _____

strong volition _____

success story _____

sunny disposition _____

supports others _____

T

tackled challenging subjects _____

team-player _____

tenacious _____

terrific interpersonal skills _____

thorough _____

tremendous drive _____

T (cont.)

tremendously talented
                                                 _____
trustworthy   _____

U

undisputed academic talents   _____
unflagging tact   _____
upbeat   _____
upbeat personality   _____
uplifting personality   _____

V

valued   _____
valued negotiator   _____
versatile   _____
vibrant spirit   _____

W

well-mannered   _____
well-traveled   _____
wholesome   _____
wide range of experiences   _____
will continue to blossom   _____
will enhance student culture   _____

Notes:

_____
_____
_____
_____
_____
_____
_____
_____
_____
_____
_____
_____